lush
poems for four voices

poems for four voices

Haidee Kruger

Protea Book House
Pretoria
2007

for jan-louis

© 2007 Haidee Kruger
First editon, first impression in 2007 by Protea Book House
PO Box 35110, Menlopark, 0102
1067 Burnett Street, Hatfield, Pretoria
8 Minni Street, Clydesdale, Pretoria
protea@intekom.co.za
www.proteaboekhuis.co.za

Editors: Gus Ferguson / Karen Horn
Cover design: Hanli Deysel
Cover image: Majak Bredell
Set in ZapfCalligr BT on 9/14.5 pt by Hanli Deysel
Printed and bound by Mills Litho, Cape Town

ISBN 978-1-86919-205-1

No part of this book may be reproduced or transmitted in any form or by any electronic or mechanical means, including photocopying and recording, or by any other information storage or retrieval system, without written permission from the publisher.

Chorus

Agnes 9
Dorothy 22
Gertrude 35
Brigid 50

Chorus

Chorus

                Oh for
a malleable woman   a jammy answer   a madonna—
pure filter imperceptible by
paper and metal, the body figmented exhaling against
the tongue like a bludgeoned rhizome,
the scalp soaked through, softened, open to
landslides   sinkholes   the drowning fall.
                Oh
for our lady of the thighs crucified
apostrophically, voice like
a bruise murmuring thou shalt thou shalt thou shalt
keep it complex   cavernous   lurid—
flesh smacking oars against black water,
the horizon a bloody rind around a sky like liver,
the finger of a saint blinking in oil.
                Yes,
thou shalt be here   not
in glory haloed with burnt sugar   not
the tattoo of eternity damasked on
your neck like dawn.
                Here. For after
is the underside of a stone:

swarming and unlit.

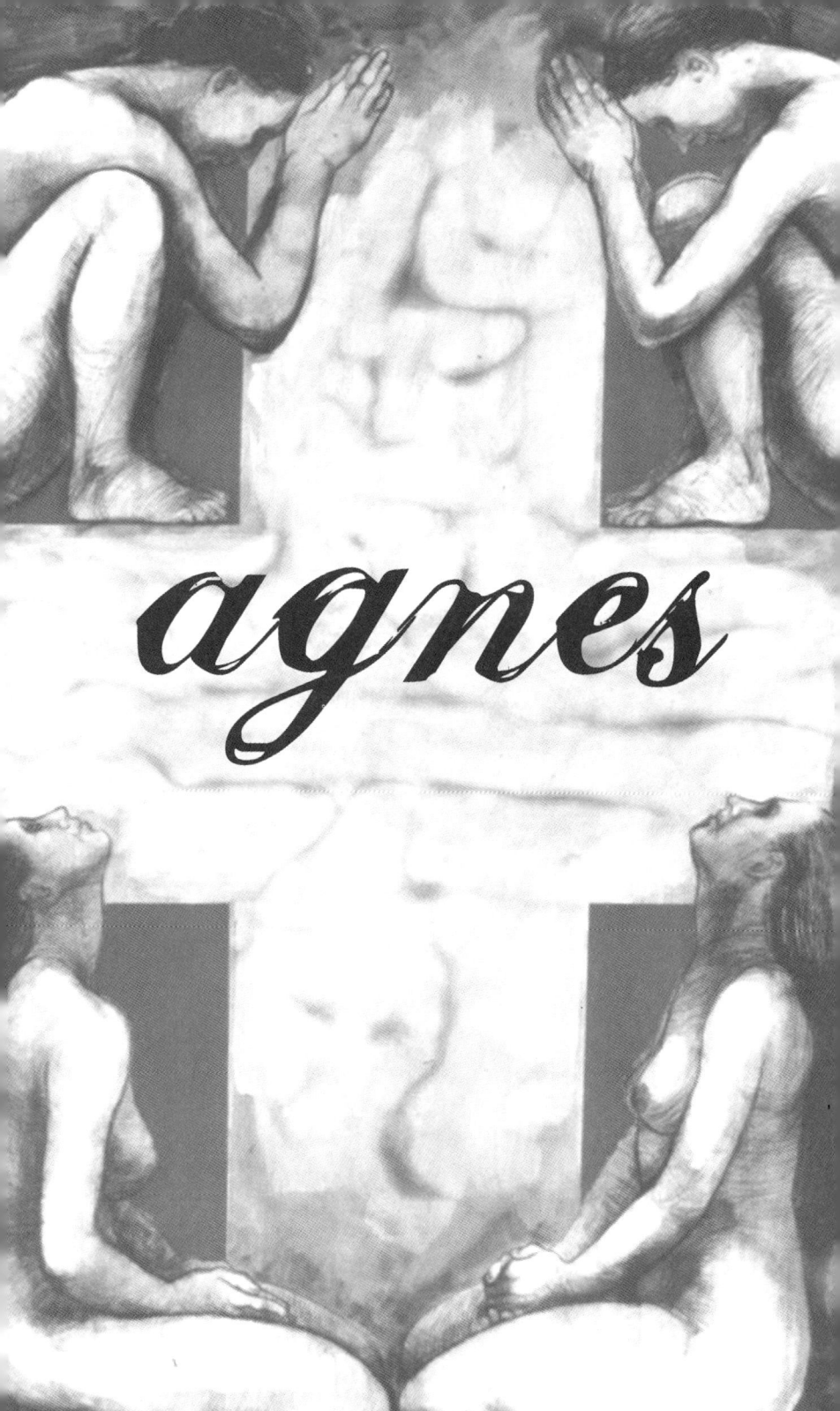

one

We go out at dawn with sharpened hands,
ready for the planting. But first
we pray, going down on hands and knees,
cheeks pressed to the mute soil, stones and brambles
cutting furrows into the skin. Mouths filled with dirt recognise
the sweetness, the surrender;
feel the seduction of the seed moving against
the tongue. We lift our palms to the sky, our fingertips
a supplication for blessing, for the supple saliva
of sun and wind and water, before returning
to the earth. We watch its barely perceptible movement, braving
the lush swirl of passion under the surface.

We are motionless, suspended;
the caress of the blade against the sky anticipating
the plunge of desire, the resonant timbre
of the coulter breaking into the blank crust:
scoring grooves of bliss to coax
a versicoloured, clamorous season
from the silence of this place.

(*verse*: from OE *fers*, from L *versus*, "a turn of the plough, a furrow, a line of writing",
from *vertere* "to turn", reinforced in ME by OFr *vers*)

two

(1)
The world watchful.
A collection of

synonyms to drive
into ahead. (Insidious

intent indeed.) To
see without saying:

a deleted machine masking
the mouth myopic,

archiving the actual.
The street armed with

women syntaxed,
soliloquies in high

heels and hotel rooms,
ribbed for whose

pleasure. The exoskeleton
of the world bruised

into a present
shimmer. Look—

the sky leaks
a litter of signs:

a flagship, a fountain,
a set of teeth, a romantic,

a climax. Oh,
not to think of a thing.

(2)
Quote. The weight
unpalatable, wrapped

in tacit dough.
Bicycles spitting

dust. The road a
lissom bride, a metallic

taste corneated. No
afterglow dumping,

no prolix prolapse linotyped
into submission. Just

a bloody balloon on
the horizon, grass crossing

swords, some spectacular
tongue. Supersized silence

lateralised, swallowed. Feet
kicking against syllabic breeze.

Swivelling back, already an
unbalanced epic erasing. Unquote.

(3)
Hanging by a
paradigmatic thread,

the world blossoms a
rotten egg. Streetlamp

by streetlamp the
tar swells to sacred.

There's something about
the armour, the way

he blinks, framing
peristalsis. Sweet

inside. Wolfwhistling and
all in green she comes.

It's a slippery
slope, by lipreading

eloped. Pulling yourself
up by the vowels. To

have many stomachs, to
stomach it. Throwing

tinted punches behind glass:
semi-coloned bliss, cloned.

three

and after

we lie
cooling
knotted and whole under
those quilts of
lopped daisies
(no longer
the terrors of
my springs) but rather

the thick molasses of
this night covering
us as

the wind comes up while
this house simmers
to life

and we

come home at
last like autumn
leaves drifting

through the
portals of our

bodies

four

  Love percolates through
sunlight bent double, oblique under
the weight of a season
that does not yet know its
name. Droplets distilled
in the sieve of desire
seep down the branches of trees, windows,
a lamppost, fossilising on my palms:
seeds of pure, quiet light reflecting
nothing but themselves.
  I open my arms wide,
and call the doves that come to eat
love from my hands. Their wings
pleat the sky as the day slowly
turns itself inside out.
  These gifts I send:
this light, these seeds, these feathers.
  Love travels.

five

swallow
me slowly
love
me to death
yes

sugar & spice
& poison & dice

that's what
little girls
are
made of

six

lay your arms down
surrender your words and
load up on love in
my bed for
seventeen minutes of
peace

—a truce
of closed eyes and
tangled limbs—

then
jump from
luminous to leaving
in one cool

shot

seven

tripping the
> razorwire trapeze in
> this circus—

balancing your
> paper cups of scalding
> words on
> pinkies with
> my eyes glued
> to the
> silver string
> that slips into
> the horizon—

hoping for
> a maybe pair
> of fins
> or a
> sunrise blue skies
> zeppelin balloon—

I have
> no hands free
> no foothold left

> nothing to defend myself

when the crows come

eight

and by the way
eve sends her regards from
somewhere beyond the great
apple of which
you too
have bitten off more
than you can
chew but
swallow swallow swallow
repeat like a mantra your
mouth full of lush full
of feathers full of milk &
honey a sky like
yolk oh

hold my
hand baby 'cause
i can see
the angel at
the gate

nine

these charms
remembered

these days
marked with

a white stone
i work into the soil

plant some
fennel and myrtle in

a circle around
your name while i

prepare to
swallow

another dayspring down
with your

silhouette

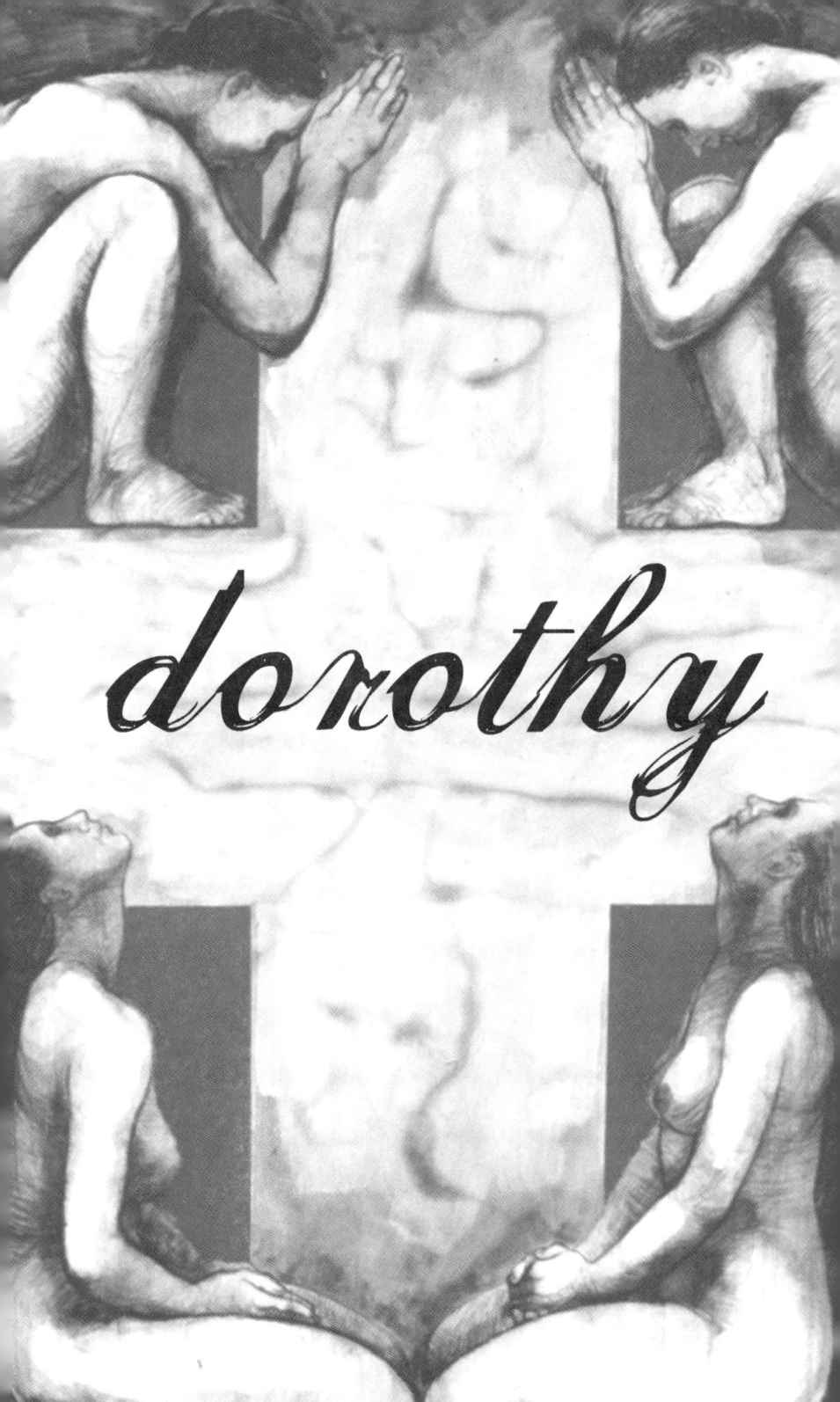

one

so long immersed
in holy water our
electric blue limb to
limb radioactive
rosary of atoms fierce like
saints on fire yes—
the arch
of your back my
oh holy grail only

to be resurrected to
half-life
silk roses and twenty-four daily
hail marys to
soothe the quiet chronic confessions
of suffocating sunsets on
a string

two

in winter here the sky
shuts down to a grey hum draped
over the rasping machinery of industry turning
like old men in cold beds:

desiccated bones shored against
the memory of mossy skin,
words slippery like avocado pips,
birth.

three

after

you retreat
like a door swinging shut &

i watch
the oblique panes of your
back folding white squares of silence
as my fingertips mutely
try to pick

your locks

four

(1)
I say

I need a heart like
a glossy suntanned seed
to pollinate the
sterile caves gaping under
my estranged skin.

you say

I think your tongue
is on fire.

(2)
I say

I feel like
a ticking clock, a rising bread,
a spoon.

you say

you are a
grater.

(3)
I say

I dream of
vermilion, pomegranate,
persimmon flesh yielding.

you say

to some extent
you are defined by lime.

five

and give us
on this
our daily planet
the witdom to elegantly
decor ate
our gaily thought
bubble gummy
noledge
falling eloquently through
space to
blankly go
where we have
all gone
before

six

in pluperfect pixilated pose we
sigh on the dotted line

tuck our britannicas into
our adverbial corsets with

our hermeneutically hoxed hymns
tied around our necks, our

brittle red hiding hoods covering
our platitudinally refraining hearts

ready to
sink or float
in shredded bliss

seven

Reality show
To go out the furthest, to gut each other, to cling to having been inspired. What they are: a kind of edge we watch, returning the brinkmanship. It's a reality room of last week's Ulysses. A show in which back to safety. But no. The very last second. The playing and playing for is the caressing closest to the verge, to catastrophe. Oh their superhero jaw lines, their perfect unscathed tits. Here Eve and Adam. Then zoom before running. Terrified of snakes. Adam tied Eve up in the closed gaze of the camera; got the most intimate with the spectacle, caressed the convex fizzle. His face in close up as episode. He can get right in and give it to her, rupture her in thousands through the lens recording their hedonistic bravery, their one-way glass. Her being bitten through the screen, we watch her struggling to. Eve is extremely true love. Out. Would dream of breathing, turning blue, passing the needle. He watched.

The ballad of unoriginal sin
No such thing as original sin. The uniqueness factory, the search for difference. But then the hidden foundation: the catalogue copied. In novels, on TV. We've created connoisseurs' couches, recognising ourselves. Maybe to inspect it, index it, buy it. For all time skinned inside unoriginal sin. Derrida: own obituary and continued hanging around regardless. I remember that spark. Ignition, recognition. One. Still. Your radar picked me up. On your desk, like seeks out like. We feed two sides into single surface. The only way of being sure that we are actually here, of being sure that we haven't missed it, springcleaning lungs, liver,

veins. Still. Between chequebooks, keys, cats, bickering, cigarettes, energy rewiring the way the brain thinks. Rectangle to Möbius strip. More, more. And the body wears the mute mechanics of it all. There is ink in your fingers, leaking. It's all there if you look closely in the shuffled light. Inside me swarm your inscriptions.

Blood
Giving it to her in its pink and crimson and scarlet, torn arteries glossing his fingertips. Tinted vermilion with sex, he swore it was hers. His eyes gave it to here, offering it. Red cells seeping into cupped hands, down her throat until she gagged. Blood, blood, blood percolating into that thing he left in her belly. His mouth is whole, because he is her completely. Like he trusted in this he needed her. He and his wrists were covered in oozing. He tore taste, pushing pores, pulsing. He wanted her to know. But. Too much. At his feet a damp mass she didn't want. And it fell at his bones so she spat his heart out beautifully. He took it and left. He left the red of poinsettias of his blood in her. Just as poisonous. It remained closer and closer, stubbornly on her tongue. Lemons did not want to let it go clean, or parsley or holy water. She tried everything, rinsing, but still. It lived in her, strange to her body. It. Kill it, abort it. But taste his mouth. And in surprise he tried to show her the days and months after.

eight

Which of an any wind blew
over down our white house gone?
What of a black fly chewed
through all of our sapling sun?
Why if any of a heart
are we hiding up our sleeve?
Who of our double hands
are lying when we breathe?
When if any of all times
did we break our hopclover soul?
Which of an any man
will help me fix it whole?

nine

daddy dear you should. be proud. your
little girl has finally
opened. her eyes wide enough
to toss a kiss at
the dingy desires of
those sweetmouthing wolves
who slither their seduction with no. shame at all
from which I crawl on hands and
knees until. finally mushroomed out
of lust and honey. darling. cream and leather I crash into
my 2am starfields garden planting
omens for posterity and smiling plastic bliss for
the cameras but. we better cut it again because. pussycat. these
surfaces are treacherous and you were bound. for a
fall anyway still. at least those stilettos sure kick
up some glamourdust buying enough time for
an escape from their. dirty claws.

so sure it is a little late I know but. damaged as
I am I must face that mirror mocking
how much. foolish child. have you sacrificed only. to
arrive here in a blue lounge of
stillborn galaxies and. halfworld dolls only. to
know you've sacrificed only. to
understand that truth doesn't grow
on trees after all and yet. to know you're
born complete for him but not
whole enough for him who
you have called your
sugar.

now here we float up and away glued to
the ceiling dodging those
derby dogs cause. I gotta get
high to find my spark. honey. while the
banshee girls wail under
my window just. keep still as
it hits then. go go go. inhale and
catch. your breath to. keep while.

the spring heist assassins leopardcrawl out of
their bunkers watch out. poppet. cause
we gotta go murder us some memories for
an anaesthetic shoot up calibrate the red of
a mars desert welling up over. ice to build
you a castle with a tall tower and
a bluebellbaby nursery instead.

so if you maybe fake yourself some
binoculars to see. forever you
might glimpse me pinning my body to
the space needles where only
turtledoves get laid and I
drift skyscraping against the
sunset like a. watchword. or
a prayer.

one

April is the cruellest month, breeding
Lilacs out of the dead land, mixing
memory and desire ...
        T. S. Eliot (The waste land)

these
branches knotted with
little green buttons
(ticking clocks)
alarming:
                    button up
                    button up

                    close
against the sewing
of new threads darning
needles mending
spry hearts   hide
desire under your dress
stuff your wanting mouth with
mould and memory until
you choke on that
thick quilt of lopped daisies: loves
me loves me
not   loves me loves me
not:

the lining of
these
days are too bright
       too soft

knitted of shifty feathers
whistling
    Sumer is icumen in
        Lhude sing, cuccu!
      Groweth sed and bloweth med
        And springeth the wude nu

but these
beaks in trees
twitch burning bluebells
stir frowns and
petty deaths died in
spoons of sugar
sweet hearts

    *

this
sky is stitched with
zigzag yellow
(running sand)
whispering:
                button up
                button up

              cover
yourself in
hat and socks and pretty beads
and laces
ready to face the stalks
        the resins
        the sun

of this:
another terrifying
glaring

spring

two

I write

in order to chaos
the light licking
unleavened skin,
to chorus compulsion
mouthing your
eyes, as

one day
blisters blindside
into the

next.

three

today
the dog dug up
the last of
your sunflowers

pity

they were getting
to be

rather beautiful

four

i smell of
    iron
    latex
    cotton
    bleach.   i taste
                    like rust.
under the sand
    my eyes are
    blanched jelly.   i will not
                        listen.
i have corrugated
    my skin against
    the brine of
    the tide.   i do not
                    speak   —there are
                                  too many
                                  sharp shells to step in
                                  in the dark.

but if you put me to
    your ear
    you will hear
    my blood
                                  howling.

five

hanging out with
    the spelunking girls honey
    going hiking going marching going
    digging through the abbey walls through the rainforests
    down into the belly of
    this place where we meet virgins and saints walking
    close behind us so
we pin our hands together dressed in
    boots and flashlights and
    blue violet dresses to confuse
    the butterfly boys who hide in trees
    waiting for a free sugar ride all
    the way to bliss and
    back baby yes
dragging picnic baskets packed
    with ice-cream and tequila to
    feed us through the
    hungry deserts and flash flood valleys we tramp our
    own secret little crusades
    whistling hallelujahs and christmas carols
    ringing bells holding hands to
    scare away the dark where swampy monsters
    hiss and steam and snarl and we are
going down so far going in so deep that
    there is no up or down
    just here and now where
    we go to bury the not yet
    children with
    the sin-eaters waiting the nuns praying

standing around your quiet
    almost shape we all
    sing holy holy for your soul and
    mine too while we
    eat the bread and salt to swallow up our
    sins together chanting for salvation but

ursula my dear if
    11 000 virgins weren't enough to
    make it through
    back then

how will i?

six

soon
i will set out
with stilts and spells
maybe an axe

soon

seven

I missed our first
obituary—

deceptively bland
typeset tattooed on
a grey season in which

my once slippery anemone skin
bloomed into ash.

We shed cinders as we drifted
down the corridors of
our shells, we bled

leaden pools
of salt into
our shoes.

Our fires
fossilised into
charcoal and chalk and

after I would spend days sweeping
up the dust while
we crumbled
and slowly ebbed
onto our brittle soundless
shores.

Haunted by
the taste of
ruby, shrieking pyres
of pigment scouring
the heart,

I know

it's time to
close the doors on our
mute and barren wastes and
send in
the hurricanes,

time to plant a goodbye kiss on our eyes,
close the coffin

and throw the first fistful
of farewell.

eight

once we were

an inertia real
weighted to
pale beds dreaming
slow like cream but

here
in this place
the trees convulse in
purple
against a sky
too fierce already
& as i pass
through this street
in this season
i am lassoed
by my too white
reflection folded like a strange quiet
paper bird in between the
shrieking traffic & suddenly
i know
here
in this place
there is a world that spins
like ballerinas on acid:

kicking & screaming i
am dragged out of my
mute anaemic glory hole while
inertia reels
before
the rush &

icollideincolour

nine

Coming to the end of a paragraph I

release,

uncurl my eyes towards
the cottonseedlight of this afternoon and

despite

the caustic margins of
season and type,
the deadend bookends of sentences swinging

shut

behind me, I come to my senses—
ambushed by the holy
procession of the future flowering unexpectedly over
the bare skin of

winter.

one

Let it vault high against
a ceiling. Let there

be bells thawing
copper sound over
a grey sky. Let it

be empty, yet
heavy like a woman with
child. Let there

be absence.

Let life hinge
unexpectedly

on every syllable.

two

you are small
here   you
are light reflecting off
the dust of
time   a surprise
second sifting
into itself
:
feel the fault lines of
your life shift   watch
the skyline change
shape   the leaves fall
and know
there is movement
beneath
:
seasons change

three

Scrabbling through the morning
what remains are
myopic mosaics of
subway stations, cellos,
the flavour of endless
rain against the tongue—
cobbled threads unravelling into
the horizon.

Scribbling through the morning I
rewind, remind,
repair the warp and
weft of
us,

composed through the lens
of your mouth.

four

marooned on mono
soundclips strut like
virgins on mescaline parading
their madrigals for a
pyromaniac future but

surprised by stereo
fledgling mantras unfold like
the cool quiet tendrils
of this green age
inside.

five

i blinked and
suddenly the starpuzzles flipped just
so   bones synchronised   & the tide
rushed inoutoveroh
oh   & you   oh you love
darted into view   my little
slippery silver sardine   &
the psychedelic angel hearse parked outside
the doors   the cherubs waved
hallelujah flags   while the midwives collected
mementos of this sweet
glorious drizzleday   & i washed

the monsoon from my eyes   the salt from
my thighs   put on my
ohholyday best &
said
hi

six

So little honey,
your mommy
doesn't drive a Chevrolet.
She hides in her closet when the wind blows,
when the girl scouts call with
cookies and milk.
She's an iambic insomniac who
throws midwinter tantrums
even when it's fiesta season,
a sucker for incognito
who's occasionally had to sing for
her tacos under
a violent concrete sky.

But she knows where
she belongs
now,

and she knows
how to make shadow puppets,
build a kite,
plant lavender and love,
grow quiet.

She is
a renowned slayer of monsters,
a follower of fairies,
an apprentice of passion.

She knows autumn,

and so
will you.

seven

my
little
éclair

folds the sky
blue like

a psalm

laughs at the
way the

clouds crease

and i turn

inside
out

for her

eight

ladies and gentlemen—
let me
introduce

myself:

for years
the girl without
the voice
    miming
    maiming
millions of meek hygienic
words without
sound

graduating to
soul writer for
the graveyard gazette
    hunted
    haunted
mellow drama
queen howling in
lurid apocalypse
script

now

just a girl

with a blunt pencil between
her fingers and
the self-inflicted
unpoetic scars of
paper cuts across
her wrists

nine

if you strip it.   no
matter whether.   like sequins
under halogen.   highs sequenced.   like
wedded.   bliss weeding down
to familiar.   ground the scent
of naked.   sticks fixes throwing.   each other's
famine switches thaumatrope.   swatches roped to
skin.   if you strip it.

[timespacebodylove]

you will find.   inside
the word.   beating.

Chorus

Soon

six hands full, all
to celebrate. For that,

something

orange and crushed, breathing
the shape of damp grass,

something

to give, to swallow, offering
thanks for your body.

Something

clean: an apple core, a washed foot,
arms white creases in the dark.

Something

to speak rivers, stairs, birth,
highways, trees, home.

Some thing

with the contours
of keeping.

Acknowledgements

The following poems first appeared in print journals and online, under different titles and in sometimes slightly different forms.

Botsotso online (www.botsotso.org.za): Agnes five, Gertrude four, Gertrude eight, Brigid eight.

Carapace 62, March 2007: Gertrude three.

Englishes: Letterature Inglesi Contemporanee, 25(9), 2005: Agnes one, Dorothy four, Dorothy six, Gertrude nine.

Fidelities XIII, October 2006: Agnes eight.

Green Dragon 4, 2006: Brigid five.

Green Dragon 5, 2007: Agnes seven.

Literator 27(1), April 2006: Brigid one.

Literator 21(3), November 2000: Dorothy nine, Gertrude five.

Litnet (www.litnet.co.za): Agnes two, Dorothy one, Dorothy four, Dorothy six, Gertrude seven, Brigid three, Brigid seven, Brigid nine, Chorus.

sweet magazine (www.sweetmagazine.co.za): Dorothy seven.